Erin Hoover's second collec
sobering effect of encounte
'80s. These poems deal in reality, eschewing the fantastic. I, a
recovering surrealism addict, am reminded of what it means to be
a writer, woman, and mother poet trying to survive this era: "I
bared / polished teeth and told the faculty in assertive yet / modu-
lated tones that I could teach anything." Having long played by
rules so detrimental to her selfhood, the speaker of these poems
shares her unvarnished truth: "I want to be able to talk to people /
without having to f-- or be f--ed, yeah?" Hell, yeah. This is a
deeply intellectual and expertly wrought collection.
—**Cate Marvin**

In *No Spare People*'s very first poem, Erin Hoover writes: "women
don't give up our creative / selves, no child demands it, / but we are
made to concede / by real people who benefit from all we relin-
quish." That searching interrogation of who and what profits from
our rhetorical and cultural passivity is everywhere apparent in this
unforgettable collection. So too is that most precious and enviable
poetic superpower—the ability to make deep love feel new,
unprecedented. Hoover writes, "Before you lived, I lived inside my
own / loathing. Some parents have children to replace / them-
selves, but we're two instead of none." These are hard poems in that
they press far past the facile reductive binaries of good and evil,
savior and saved, and into something—a lyric, a voice—that feels a
little more complicated, a little more like our own world.
—**Kaveh Akbar**

In the mother-daughter family of *No Spare People*, everyone is essential—one parent, one child—with truly no one to spare. This collection explores the difficulties of such economy within our particular economy, in which "deprivation will make you zealous." Yet the poems do not give up, continually questioning the constraints of an American South in which "some days, I'm the pioneer wife, / keeper of the homestead, but others / I'm absurdly educated for a uterus." Erin Hoover's *No Spare People* is an indelible record of the pleasure and power of a woman's choice to have and raise a child on her own.

—Jessica Jacobs

I'm a long admirer of Erin Hoover's work. At its absolute best, poetry enlarges the people, places, and things it zooms in on. The poems in *No Spare People* illuminate the injustices of income inequality, misogyny, womanhood, and motherhood in America with an expanse of time and geography. The voices of these poems arrive at their questions and epiphanies through vivid and self-aware language: "It is tempting to want always to reduce the thing to its detail. To make it small." Read this book. Expand.

—K. Iver

No Spare People

poems

ERIN HOOVER

www.blacklawrence.com

Executive Editor: Diane Goettel
Book Design: Amy Freels
Cover Design: Zoe Norvell
Cover Art: "Call is waiting" by Ever Baldwin. Courtesy of Ever Baldwin and
Marinaro, New York. Photo credit: Matt Grubb, New York.

Published 2023 by Black Lawrence Press.
Printed in the United States.

Contents

"Our feminist politics makes things as well as breaks things."
—Sara Ahmed

"Begin with the material."
—Adrienne Rich

I.

On the metaphor, for women, of birthing to creative activity

I was trying to explain that transposition
between having thoughts and doing for others,
because in every household the metaphor is clear:
the caretaker is a woman, and so
                    when I began
writing, I listed out my morning, the preparations
and cleaning up of spills and toys, taking down
and fetching, the driving and carrying of people
that no one wants to know about
if we believe in the reality of book contracts
and job offers. I had
                    an accomplished list,
I believed, a specific and authentic record
of the drain cleared, of stirring a pot
and rubbing the back of a hysterical child,
and through it I thought I constructed
a breathing replica of my life, the aspic
in which I moved. But when I looked inside,
looked closer, I found only
                    the second-wave woman,
nearly the very same image I knew repeatedly
as a girl and as a woman trying to write,
you are not this,
                    you are *this*,
these binaries, again and again. Yes, my time
was missing, I did not sleep very much then,
I had ground myself down on the mill wheel
of uncompensated work, but my thoughts

beat batwings against my skull, some of them
more powerful than any idea
I'd had yet in my life. I even wrote down
all the things that flapped out of me at night
in hours I stole from sleep or was expected to use
on my child. I wrote the way writing feels urgent
when you learn energy has been expended
to silence you, or worse,

                                    to get you to silence
yourself. These ideas that I wrote
and even tried to publish were utterly
new to me, I couldn't have known them except
for motherhood, and I wrote like this for years
to an audience performing the great labor
of the world, not only women but so many of us,
we who are asked not to consider aloud

                                    what we become inside
our prisons, schools, hospitals,
our profitable, dick-swinging offices,
we who are asked and then silenced by force,
reduced pay and firings, dwindled invitations
and the refusal of our words, belittled by stories
everyone else seems to sign on for
that tell us to disbelieve our lying eyes.
In the midst of my work, running another errand
or in the middle of the night, I wrote through it,
learning women don't give up our creative
selves, no child demands it,

                                    but we are made to concede
by real people who benefit from all we relinquish,
those we know personally and those agents
of power who do their best to be invisible,
and then we are told this uncreative life

was a choice. The list I made on the day
I found a dead mouse under the sink
and buried him, when I tore apart
my child's jigsaw puzzle in a glorious flying out
of edges and fixed our washing machine
with my own weary hands, it told me how angry
I was at these tasks, a barrage I believed
had worn my mind smooth. It explained
why the writing came in pieces
but the list was not what I wanted to say,
                          that I experience joy
because I have made room for it. I am writing
that while the metaphor, for me,
of birthing to creative activity
is in some ways correct, it is only the first move
to conjure a woman's grievances,
and it is past time to make the second, and so
                          I ask her to speak,
                          I call her forth,
                          I open my throat.

At the child support office

the children were surprisingly calm. Later I'd learn
what my own child would accept, grown used
to our nomadic life, but that was years away. Barely

a person at two weeks, unlike me, she couldn't focus
on the men shuffling to the window to murmur
words like *cohabitate* instead of what I would say,

lived with, *paternity* instead of father. I understood
that the men used legal rather than familial words
because we were in an open-plan, echoing room

that wasn't about families at all. I too had come
to make a declaration, that my baby was mine alone.
At my turn, the clerk asked if I had proof, and I looked

down at the fold of my child's mouth, her animal
hands. I felt the diaper that held together my body
ripped open not long before—I could hardly walk—

but maybe that only proved, like her birth certificate,
that I was her mother. You can't prove a negative,
I wanted to say, but the nurse taking blood

in the corner of the room wanted that, the man
with his sleeve rolled up wanted it too. *I see a father
listed*, the clerk said, and told me a French name,

man piloting a swamp boat through my imagination.
A stranger who, peering under our car seat bonnet,
would be as confused as I am at how the State of Florida

found a husband for me. Clerical error of a man.
In response, I supplied the Latinate words that conjured
my baby, *artificial insemination*, for all to hear,

handing over the letter I asked my doctor to write.
My word, I had to do that, get a letter like that.
I've learned that I can't tell people what they don't

already believe, but I fought for that blank space.
This isn't a confession but the facts that surround us,
as everyone has, and once my child's fake father was gone,

I thanked the clerk and ran through the parking lot
through the gathered, hissing geese. I drove home,
opened my shirt, and on that spring day, fed my child.

Homewrecker

You'd have to understand the home
        as a unified construct, as a guarded entity,
locked up like a bank vault, a virgin,
        or like a rarified set of collectible dolls
with no inherent value but worth agreed
        upon. You'd have to really
buy into that,
        the quality of the dolls' cornsilk hair,
or wee fingernails painted with real polish,
        the hardscrabble factory in Minnesota
where Slovenian immigrants hand-sewed
        their 100% cotton gowns half a century
before your husband was born. You'd need
        to assume that a man
could be as pliant as one of these plastic,
        factory-built objects, his limbs
grooved to only move certain ways,
        careful turning the head as it's liable
to snap off with enough hard twisting.
        Do you, personally, know a particular
man like this, a vessel, or will any man do
        whose attention turns lightly on a thick,
nearby thumb, are you lucky to seize
        such an empty wisp of a man, to grip tight
to that vacancy and hold fast,
        you good girl?

Maternity exhibit in an election year

It was one of the wars we marched against, I was marching—
no, this was before the march, I was volunteering. I made calls
for our candidate from a yurt at the land cooperative,
driving Miccosukee out of town, no shoulder, late at night,
my brights flashing against red possum eyes, I kept thinking,
I'll die out here, I'm pregnant,

we'll die. All of the co-op women looked like the nominee,
an older white lady, but she was the first white lady
to run, back when a woman winning still
seemed possible. I told the co-op women that I didn't speak Spanish
so they gave me calls in the Black side of segregated Orlando,
still plenty of Spanish-speakers, and I tried to dig in

and root myself there, to wear the exasperation of people
I called at dinner who didn't live in yurts, swearing up and down
they didn't know about any election, their concerns
for everything in their lives but this not
exactly shocking. People humored me as I went on
about locating their polling place, and—I swear—

the script I got at the co-op wanted me to explain democracy
as a concept, as in, *This candidate is the vehicle
for what you believe*, but I threw that out, I don't talk down to people,
not that way. No one was planning to vote,
and I knew months before the polls closed their outcome
although I still didn't grasp the implications of our failure—

I say *our* because I too saw our candidate's victory as inevitable,
though years later I don't begin to believe
anyone really thought we'd take a battleground where, history tells us,
you've got to sweep to win at all. But that night
for the first time another person saw me
without me having to say it, one of the granny organizers

with miraculous thick hair, that long gray hair exclusive
to co-op women, bathed in argan oil and peppermint, worn
down to the waist as a birthright. She asked how I was coming along.
You mean the calls? She replied, *No, the baby.* She was the first
to identify me as a mother, not knowing much else
about me but that I was her kind. As her eyes went liquid,

she opened her posture in welcome, her shoulders and arms an O
at the newly-round letter of my body, and the deep void at its center filling,
filling up, I said: *coming along fine.* In a strange yurt and a misguided
campaign I allowed my inner hope to turn outward, at last owning
the identity I wear now instead of any other dawning
that seeped into our habitat on the circuitous road home.

The hedge fund manager's first wife

I have been in her house. Not the second
wife but the former publicity boss
who was, everyone acknowledged,
prettier than her husband. In a bouquet
of white roses, I was the ruscus. I traded
my labor for wages. I wasn't bleeding,
but I wore a tampon to sit on her
white couch. She chaired the gala event
for my employer, a charity. One day
the hedge fund manager and his second wife
would pose for reporters behind a sheet
of dollar bills, uncut Washington
green. But this was then. Inherited
New York money bought their pirate ship
of windows floating 300 feet above
Park Avenue. It bought our charity,
our group of women, and me, nearly
lowest of all. I dared not speak. A person
tiered beneath me had arranged
plates of canapés and fruit on the table
to later clear away whole, her work
accomplished between the ticks
of the clock. I tried to feel her presence,
invisible like my own, while the first wife
told us our ads should be in *Town and Country*,
Vogue, the Hamptons mags. The right
people, she said, couldn't see us. I imagined
my life as her cat, weaving its body
around the clawed feet of her living room

table, my life as her table, polished
but otherwise unobserved. I'm not jealous
of any wife clinging to what ownership
she knew, nor of the hedge fund manager
in his capital-blue suit, who when asked
to serve a god even lower than money would
move, second wife on his arm, into place.

The nineties

Some of us long for the hypocrisy again.
—Arundhati Roy

We gathered in mall atriums, smudged
our gum under benches. Around us,
our leaders unleashed markets yearning
to breathe free. I skulked outside
the candle store. I wanted a boyfriend
with long, straight hair like a girl, wanted
punk rock and to be called feminist,
not Dr. Hill's testimony mocked
by macho senators, but three chords
and copyshop zines. Our history books

ended at D-Day and we made up the rest,
mourned animals whose stuffed replicas
cluttered our bedrooms. Some believed
in the necessity of a planet, others
practiced easy detachment. Our problems
were one-note, easily reckoned, the poetry
of CFCs and acid rain and the opaque
beige skyline of L.A. We caught national
abuses on video, like granular tape
of police baton-beating a Black man

prone on the ground, evidence I saw
and didn't see every day. On Wall Street,
extremists blasted a hole at the base
of our tallest shrines, smoke twisted skyward
and the tag "radical Islamic terrorists"
wormed into our minds like advertising.

Oh, we'd hear it again. By pen stroke
our nation joined the largest free market
in the world. We couldn't see sweatshops,
didn't even try, as retail spaces filled

with bright, cheap objects. Untraveled outside
our great white middle, I was impressed
by unlimited salad and breadsticks.
I babysat kids who raised leaden soldiers
to their mouths as our parents attended
their last union meetings. At the doctor,
insurance paid. Good teeth, good shoes,
good psych drugs, the last mild summer
before wildfire. We watched as cynics
stripped the welfare state, like pulling down

the walls of someone else's house to rip
out the fixtures as they tried to live inside.
I spent my grandma's social security
on compact discs and retro housewife
dresses, I ate burritos and mini
microwave bagels decorated to look
like pizzas. No one asked more from me,
yet I was dissatisfied. To live then
was like hitting a drug, all consequences
saved for another day. On the prairie

a veteran blew a federal building
wide open, children inside. The paper
printed the word "penis" for the first time,
and we gawped at Lorena and Tonya,
aired the O.J. verdict in French class.
Clerks shot up mailrooms, workplace

shootings morphed into teenaged boys
decked out with semiautomatics,
the trench-coat myth easier to buy
than the thrall of guns on tap. The dot-com

bubble became the housing bubble
turned to this festering boil we live inside
but haven't named. Like some others,
I had a modem that screamed into
the night. In chat rooms, I told strangers
my intimate personal details, spoke deeply
about my core beliefs, and that benign
audience, both transparently decent
and brand new at this, put the data
to no use. The Internet that would change

our human synapses had awakened,
but this wasn't its ascendency. Not yet,
as we persisted in trading real goods, real
services, real dollars. I knew how much cash
I carried. The court convicted one doctor
for euthanizing the ill while others
delivered patients to amber-bottle narcotic
death. I wanted a girlfriend. I wanted
to learn about Marxism at a college
to bankrupt my parents. Across the world,

future autocrats scrounged blood lucre
melted off colonial skeletons,
flattered over caviar, dug in their heels.
Always rubles and riyals to be made,
always another dollar. Imagine how
confident we felt in our unquestioned

virtue, how we shied from the webcam,
our future closer than it appeared.
We hugged our own hollow surfaces.
We would never be this perfect again.

Three weeks

The most famous athlete
in the country wanted you as he
wanted many women,
but then, he wanted you
more, that elite gloss to your hair
and skin, photogenic emblem
of where you came from
and where you'd go,
Nicole, you pink-skied Los Angeles
of possibility, not his wife
but you. More than anything,

you were young
in those three weeks
between the day you finished school
and your first club shift,
all spray tan and Hash jeans,
in the days and hours you weren't
yet with him but alone.
After that, did your mind
ever quiet, did you stop considering
him and think about yourself?
Because I can tell you where I was

in that thin cut of time
when like you I didn't belong
to anyone, riding in the Chevy Malibu
of an 18-year-old boy. *An adult,*
I whispered to my friends.

I was 15 and I couldn't stand my face
in photographs, so none exist,
but people would have called me pretty,
no ice queen—not like you—
a girl lukewarm and unchic
though as perishable
under the right
circumstance. In 1994

June was no different
than in every year prior or since.
In evening the stupid moon hung
in the stupid sky even with the sun
shining, the piece of earth we knew
closer to the sun than it would be
nearly all year. I was in his car,
school was out and the whole day
felt like squinting through
the hot, greasy dust on a windshield.
Earlier that day, alone,
I cut my nails too short out of boredom,
binged mint ice cream out of boredom,
I waxed nonexistent hair from
my upper lip. I never thought
about myself because like you,

I was the culmination
of every falsehood I'd been taught,
the days whipping by me
as I willed my time to run out,
I was that close to feeling loved,
but that night, Nicole,

we turned on the radio
and your husband had realigned
your murder story to his own orbit.
He threatened to shoot himself
zooming down the freeway—
or crawling, as it appeared to us
from the eye of a helicopter. Slow.
Penitent. It was like any of the cop shows
we watched to teach us about danger.
I'd like to say I learned that day
about men who don't think women
are people at all,

but I already knew, all over the country,
girls like me knew.

Death parade

Once I had a boyfriend from Kentucky who liked to hear me talk: *Tell me about 9/11 again.* An English professor in training, he didn't believe the disaster was a big deal outside of its rhetorical possibilities.

It is easier to believe in the look of an object than in the object. For instance, he scouted eBay for replicas of the black patent boots the Kentucky state police had issued to his father during the strike in Harlan County. They looked French, in the way certain high-fashion cuts sometimes trickle down to the mass market.

**

Every so often, I try again to find that post-9/11 air.

Back then, I lived with an asthmatic roommate on Thirteenth Street and both of us waitressed at a cafe outside Beth Israel. I mostly remember talking about the air with my roommate and other people at the cafe. Letting a day pass without talking about the smell of the air felt wrong, and yet to do so now approaches cliché, decades later when 9/11 has been so thoroughly discussed.

**

According to scientists, when a memory includes vivid details, we feel confident about it, but most of these "flashbulb" memories are not accurate.

**

Reiterating my memories of 9/11 hardens them, separates me from them, while I want to move closer, to turpentine away their finish.

In the restaurant where I worked, a paramedic asked me if I knew what we were breathing in. I said I'd read it was the contents of the WTC, filing cabinets and computers charred and transformed into tiny particles. *Bodies, too,* she said. *The buildings contained people.* I wept at the time, but when I share that anecdote, it enters the minds of others and means less to me.

**

The terrors of years ago have quit offering useful advice.

When I was a kid, everyone talked about Love Canal as a toxic dumping ground, or radiation from Three Mile Island, and today no one talks about either.

**

Now the coronavirus has arrived. It was always going to arrive; it was predicted, like 9/11.

**

A parade is a string of symbols, but a parade is also a display of power, prosperity, or the national mood, the definition of each being a matter of control.

Several summers ago, I attended the sesquicentennial of my small hometown, a parade of cars with the tops down, fire engines, dignitaries throwing hard candy into the street. One man dressed like Abraham Lincoln, complete with stovetop hat made of paper mache. He sauntered down our main street on stilted boots, tossing candy.

I can't see the sidewalk in front of my old apartment, and I can't picture the walkway leading to the house I live in now. I do have the memory of every kid in town shoulder to shoulder at the curb, crouching in the sun, anxious for those boring butterscotch candies to ricochet off the pavement, toward their small waiting hands.

**

People didn't have kids after 9/11, and so there are fewer adults of college age today. This is one of the facts distressing my field, higher education. The pandemic is another.

At first the pandemic was all of the things we couldn't have. Then it just was. A cough was a harbinger of death. Then, it was a cough.

I phoned friends still living in New York, losing their minds for any reason besides the cold-storage morgue trucks parked outside the hospital. *She didn't do the dishes. She left out the margarine.* On the news, a commentator called the numbers on our screen, the uptick in fatalities, a death parade.

I live in one of the states that didn't close down. I got on videochat with a local friend who had the virus, delirious, rasping that she'd see me soon. She was the one struggling, but I couldn't stand to look at her pretend everything was all right. Her sunken posture in the recliner and the fever shining through her skin, that is inside me now. Will I keep it?

**

It is tempting to want always to reduce the thing to its detail. To make it small.

That morning I wore heels, and because I had to walk forty blocks that day, I no longer wear them, I said for the first time a year after 9/11 at an event commemorating the cataclysm. I don't remember the walk home at all, but I would say it again and again.

If I wear glasses, will you be able to see me?

When I was a child, always my aunt stood in the center of rooms, buttoned into tennis whites or an off-the-shoulder dress, her red-tipped fingers tilting back a long-stemmed wine glass, her laughter a hoot. I thought instead of working, she chose long hours at the gym or shopping, driven from place to place by my uncle in their luxury American car. My aunt listened to books on tape from the library and signed birthday cards with erratic loops. She made her way past the room's furniture without help and looked in the direction of the person speaking. My brother told me she was reading lips, a transposition. I haven't inherited her condition, which runs in families, but even so, I strain with lenses and I have almost no night vision at all. Labs precisely calibrate my glasses, a costly process taking months. When technology dulls a problem, it isn't a problem. "I've never seen a prescription like yours, *har-de-har-har!*" People imagine I'm curious, squinting at hello, leaning in as if to kiss the document in my hands. A doctor once diagnosed me as "clumsy," not a medical condition but a scold. At night, I've pointed my car at a direction I believed to be a road, just as my aunt used to turn toward my voice. When I truly can't see, I cry out. Since I watched my aunt I've learned some cries are like talismans, some kinds of laughter, too. They guard against all the ways it can get worse. You learn to feel your way: a page of text, a conversation, a city, a museum of impressionist paintings. I'm more attentive to shifts in shadow and light than I used to be, when my eyes were better. My mind performs the calibrations now. Are you still having trouble? Maybe I'm not recognizable at all.

Apartment home in Florida as failure of the imagination

When you first came here, you loved
the outlaw construction,
the way all the men seemed to carry a knife
in the boot. It was wild, wasn't it?
Calculating all the trajectories of trees
relative to your parked car, learning as you did,
by the time the schools call out
you best scramble for any battery
and check what it fits later. During the storm,
you were grateful for few, narrow windows,
to notch your eye to a glass slat
like a minor parking-lot god.
Dependent for once on your own
sense, instead of the TV (gone out),
the cell tower (busted).
Only after, in weeks of recovery,
in the unnetworked darkness
you see how ugly this place was built,
how its cement corners depend on electric
light. You sleep in the hot night,
hot part of the world during
its hot time. You are too old for this.
You store your food in a damp cloth,
you wring out clothes
in the pit of your sink. Should you drive,
you find militarized streets,
service station lines, caravans of linemen
and National Guard. Your training,
it was never the right kind.

In these moments you see.
So consumed were you
with the small mechanics of survival
within an all-devouring premise,
you realize, the premise was all wrong.
You do not have to exhaust your surroundings.
In equilibrium with the earth,
in a pleasant and kind backdrop,
gratitude might pulse through you.
But that possibility you will forget once
power is restored.
Deprivation will make you zealous,
your celebration worthy of feasting,
of meat and milk, the pulses of animals
only recently stilled, cold and plentiful
juices, Publix's wide and deep
bounty. It was wild, that life,
wasn't it?
You had so many choices.
You had so few.

Self-owning rondeau

Willingly I drop into an online oubliette
each night. Easeful outer gleam, inner stuff
flavored by rage. Its passage bitter
but wine-smoothed. Audience I can't see, twist
of insight—I'm a genius—before ruin. Careful

shutting the hatch. Get away from my hubby,
they say. One star, they say. Sardonic
hot takes by verified poets, clique-bait
Guggenheims. Jumped into the hellmouth willingly,

on purpose, and how should I act now, coif
on fire? They say don't feed the trolls, but enough,
silence invites violence, every nerd knows this.
I'm a child here, and getting younger. Trolls slip
from the woodwork, snap at my baby knuckles.
I never willingly wanted this oubliette.

The power of passive voice

On a news loop, the FBI director crossed
the Blue Room, his face arranged
in a recursive "oh shit" expression, like
my questions of what to do, how to act,

now that this man is president. I know
my own grandiosity, I am no patriot, and
on that day, I drank house merlot,
unemployed Florida parent drowning in

terrifying but common quicksand. Even as
the Watergate lawyers cited, again,
a new and historic end to precedent,
that afternoon, the security-cleared translator

called Reality Winner had already left work
at the Whitelaw Building in Augusta,
report on Russian election interference
stuffed in her tights. Or should I say

the file *was printed* and *was removed*
from a facility, *was sent* to a journalist,
a chimera appearing by invisible hand
before us, because who was Reality Winner

but our collective, passive-voiced American
conscience, too naive not to breadcrumb
her own espionage conviction? The passive
can be a change agent that obscures

responsibility, might even enable action, but
we know how it's used in this country,
because Reality Winner is in prison and
everyone else in this story walks free. I suspect

she wanted what I had, a version of family,
my anonymous face frozen in the TV strobe,
all my Lean Cuisines and breastfeeds and job
applications. Where each day is an

exercise in additive futility, concealed
by believing so hard in it. At her arrest,
CNN used an aerial of the federal building
where our offhand mole once worked, all

fluid lines, walkways paved into a series of
curves. The planners might've pictured
ocean waves, a current in which to lose
ourselves, day after day of the relentless

neutrality of water as it slips through
so many fingers, strong-armed
double H joined to a single culpable O
shaped like a needle's eye.

Praying inside the emergency

Ladies of Pyrex and cornucopias,
we meet in the evening,

in circled chairs and cradling
leather Bibles. We open our arms

to hug, breath sweet and tart
as a cooled mug of tea. Our meeting

is long and about Jesus,
and I marvel how his parables land

close to my ear, not exactly,
but I mistrust perfection. When

one of us asks for prayer concerns,
at first we look at our hands

and feet, those body parts
crafted for earthly labor,

but then at last we name them,
the illness fresh or ongoing,

the errant cell, the off-tempo heart.
We pray for consults and MRIs,

for children launching off precipices,
their panic attacks and their

contraband, our kids who are
suckers for every kind of pain,

pain and its sucking sound against
their candied child-hearts. As though

in speaking our intentions
to each other we talk to God,

we pray for diabetic coworkers,
the neighbor whose Alzheimer's

stole his language, Chile, the Congo,
for pain felt a hemisphere away,

and finally, the kin of people
who have died in car accidents

in our town and on our roads—
pain's purest signifier, Grade-A

sweet pain, edge of the cut pain,
the sick roulette of a Tuesday.

I'm alive, and after this prayer
ends, I pray my bones won't

obstinately crack on every hard
surface in town, bucolic lampposts

demanding my sacrifice,
half-whisper of my prayer

hemming me toward the buzz
of those praying for me,

as though by speaking my own fears,
I manifest them. I pray, a speck

too scientific to believe in prayer
as more than mass hallucination,

the way ancient people offered herbs,
tokens, the fine-boned carcasses

of birds, imagined an entity
to collect them. I pray because

I can't bend social orders
let alone my own diminutive life

to my will, and I have bent so hard
that I broke myself, on protest

and on that most ethereal of wishes,
the vote. Instead of God, then

I pled with all of humanity. Now
I perform small charities, like not

being a shit in what ways the day
offers. I pray, and in my prayer admit

that in every hardship, to act
might take the form of rage, but

also joy, blinking in the heated room,
the snarl of someone's stomach,

an Amen for every improbable
holy body. I pray, may we rise.

Retail requiem

Requiem for Ames, markdown chain rolling
high through the eighties, for fading brands
bought up and Frankenstein-fused, for stores
finally shuttered, their doors pasted with bright
commands, everything must go. Requiem
for People's Drug, for Hills' firetruck
of a toy aisle, for the hamsters balled up
in the pet section at Woolworth's, for Hess's
junior clothes corner, all the places I knew
were sick before they died. Requiem
for Wannamaker's and G.C. Murphy, brands
whose Harrisburg fronts I glimpsed like cathedrals
from a car. Requiem for Phar-Mor, the discount
drug-shill whose rocketing growth, 300 stores
out of nowhere, turned out to be criminal,
and for that particular Phar-Mor I shopped
as a teenager, where in the makeup aisle
at the zenith of my insecurity, I learned to
sip generic diet sodas and dream. Requiem
for Encore Books and for Blockbuster Video,
those places I worked and whose registers
I know in my sleep—you haunt me. Requiem
for Montgomery Ward, grandpa that slumped
through the century but whose anchor location
in the mall had, no shit, a kick-ass electronics store,
bravely carrying on until the Christmas
the corporation called it. We mourned the old,
historic ones, Ward, Sears, we launched
their kayaks on fire, kept their corpses standing
as the analysts screamed their doom. Requiem

for family shopping day, for the trip into town,
for the blow out, the blaring commercials,
holiday discounts encircling us like hugs,
perpetual, near-constant sales, for President's
or Labor Day week, the frantic Christmas rush,
your season, Lord, for months. Requiem
for Pomeroy's, survivor of the Great Depression,
whose elegant tags I still find on inherited
clothes and furniture. For The Bon Ton,
who bought Pomeroy's and closed soon after,
including my store, whose ladies' fashion buyer
pegged my style—where is she now?—the building
still vacant, a restaurant's overflow parking lot.

Eternal rest grant them, O Lord, the businesses
begun and finished, warehouses scraped out
but aisles marked in masking tape on the floor,
the haphazard fragments of signage and shelving.
Requiem for the people we were as we loitered
through those aisles, browsed and tried on
and rung up, for our credit cards, and for the people
who unlocked the glass doors in the morning
and locked them again at closing, the people
who lost their jobs, in many cases us.

Requiem, too, for the people who made the goods
we bought, the means of production bone-close,
most likely overseas, the slashed-through
price tag signaling deals that were too neat,
slave labor, subject of Sunday news shows,
conditions we could protest if we would only agree
to see them. May we guard against those forces
shuttled through their online replacements,
may we one day understand the psychosis
that built then eroded what it built, that was us.

My generation is not lost but we are losing

In the good economy, I boarded puddle jumpers
for rural campuses, shook the hands of faculty

whose pinched mouths showed they were tired.
Dutifully, they moved me from building to building

so I could lecture their pretend students, so many
parking lots to cross, taped-off areas blocking

off landmines where other candidates had exploded.
I was a champion, the fattest and most entitled cow,

and I interviewed in person for two years. Once the bad
economy began, I learned to flatten myself

on a screen, so determined I was to survive. I bared
polished teeth and told the faculty in assertive yet

modulated tones that I could teach anything. I made
my promises to muted laughter, to faces hidden

on Zoom, while in the cities, orderlies bagged bodies
and nurses protested for masks, footage we all

watched late into the night. I couldn't sleep, either.
I began sending emails to people I knew, friends

that I imagined were better connected. They began:
I'm reaching out to see? or *Do you know*

someone who might need? but no one had time
to answer. No one could turn off the news.

Some watched the news for years straight.
Some became the news, swallowing whole

its desolation in cyclical packages of footage,
learning to frame the fracture in their own lives

as reportage. I posted volumes of stupid shit.
Agents of the state murdered George Floyd,

and I resented what I had, my disinfected
echo chamber, this performance layered

over the dead. There's a record of what I did,
days timestamped by email. How I tried.

I built pedagogy workshops as my students
gave up entirely on school. I drove to the border

of my dry county and bought a handle of vodka,
drank to blur my vision. I wanted to be as useless

as a governor. I threw my expensive
pens, my interview suit, into the open sewer

of a nearby lake. *I have alienated everyone,* I told
my family. *Imagine,* I whispered into the voicemail

of my Congressperson, *wanting to fit somewhere.*
I hadn't found my purpose. Or was it lost?

In the bathroom mirror, I made outsized vows
to become necessary. I swore, again, to be good.

II.

Visiting assistant professor

I love the bungalow
she lived in,
its porch with birdsnest
stuffed in the eaves,
its eaved porch,
sweet gum street
lined with wintry,
northern trees. Road
she walked to her work
at the college—
her gates wrought-iron,
my pine-needled paths,
the train tracks that
I, too, cross,
next to her office
with its high ceiling,
its bookless shelves I fill.
I call the other professors
colleagues, our conversation
a vessel into which
I pour water
that was once
someone else's,
this work a table
where another
supped. The days tick by
and the sense of a person
recently exited
disappears from the rooms,

and soon the students
who remember her
are gone. I hope
myself enough
to fill this place,
for two years,
for three,
my nest, my path,
this pitcher of words
I pour and pour
and pour.

White woman

The men in my state clean up, in suits
that fit and faces shorn for work,
and this place has made me prettier,
spanked the hard vowels right out
of my mouth. Every door swung open
for me, a man behind it, beaming
a question, an allowance: *ma'am?* True,
some days, I'm the pioneer wife,
keeper of the homestead, but others
I'm absurdly educated for a uterus,
afraid I'll forget how closely this place
once held water fountains as an organizing
force, still does. The Northern states
are self-satisfied, segregated too,
but here I am whiter, a white
weapon to be wielded, a pliant, powerful
fool. I've never been so queer as I am
in the South, where we're taught
to call a scrape of cells "baby, pre-born,"
like cake mix or powder cement
to be reconstituted by men. Like water,
men are everywhere, and I am a vessel
unmatched, unmarried, a chamber
to be eyed. Some Northern men
would like to handle me, too, but for now
I moderate my voice and when I get
a *ma'am* I nod my princess nod. The men
in my state clean up, and so do I,
but if "prettier" is a door to walk through,

where does it ever get me? I say
the only words safe for me to say,
thank you, beg your pardon, I lilt them
like charms as I search for my way out.

Maternity exhibit as the singularity

Let this rift

open. Measuring tape season,

belly smeared with gel
and wand pressed gently to flesh

season,
persistent *ba-bum, ba-bum* like radio

from space. Season of friends and competitors

who offer congratulations
in earnest, or glee she's ruined

her shot
at the good jobs. Season of ambiguous

notices about who will pay for the doctor,

standing in line
to fax forms to Medicaid, again.

Praying
for textbook, for according to plan,

in every way failing—doughnut glaze

depositing under fingernails,
dirty sheets, dirty house. Let the bills

rain down,
pile up, stash and hoard. Season of trying

not to read articles about stillborns

or defects or even
C-sections, woman working like she knows

when she'll die, as in every
Twilight Zone where foreknowledge

is a curse. Long hours made longer by

the body's automatic
cellular work. Season of a hand fisted

behind the back,
expression flattened to absorb every well-meant

homily about parenting, as if a woman

pregnant is a farm animal
only caring to alternate between trough

and pen. Treated as such
by doctors. How easily they could put away

a mother thought dangerous. For the baby.

Season of intense physical
loneliness, no coffee, no wine, be careful

on the stairs.
Long walks from inconvenient parking,

effort of moving a body through space.

The mother made finite,
while inside her exists any and all

unknowns, the birth
of her child its own terrific event horizon.

Soon it will be over. Let whatever comes, come.

Let this rift never close.

Proof of impossibility

A room with furniture removed   is still a room

It has its own particular   room-ness not least

of all this expanse   to move through

It took me so long to get   here

to let my skin   protect me and   stop responding

to refuse finally   to give in

or push back   Even as a girl   above me hovered

an idea of use   my body an equation   to all alike

An embarrassing number   touched me

but I see now   how few   have loved me

only considered me curious   the way I loved others

a riddle   a source of jealousy or suspicion

a fang   The anger of men I can almost

forgive   but in some circles   the women screamed

their lizard fury   Earlier in my reckoning

I would allow   that jaggedness to fill me

but my body   is no longer porous   I am no longer

what I once was   his friend

a term as antiquated as its   corresponding *dear*

as with written confidences   *Dear Sir* or *Dear Madam*

so close to darling   and so far   Half-morsel

the only word for us   when for a moment

another saw in me   an exact match to myself

Real Arkansas

It's easy in the South not to get invited
anywhere, hard as a dime to parse
public niceties from the truer,
private kind, a BBQ where I can join

the conversation. Not everyone is the same,
bellowing to hang their senators,
living and dying by the Hellenistic tragedy
of SEC football—though some do—

so I agree to a four-year-old's birthday
with my daughter, who like most kids
beats her parent at making friends. Driving,
I set my pilgrim sail to alien coordinates,

geography whose stories I know are bad:
race massacres, rebel graveyards,
the tear-down plantation where the county
was founded next door to my apartment,

swimming pool and central air on land
worked by two hundred in bondage.
Nobody ever tells you how stunning
the canopy is, breeze pulling a long, bright coat,

the landscape a terrifying Eden. Why not
serve hot dogs stacked in a giant bowl
like disordered Lincoln Logs,
rip our buns from grocery plastic,

eat on the couch surrounded by big dogs
and babies as outside our kids jump
on a trampoline? No reason but these people
aren't mine. We're so glad you're here,

one lady says to me. *You're punching down,*
I hear a poet friend whisper at me
ten years ago. The place I came from
isn't perfect, and some call it notorious,

Yankee town hung with confederate flags,
full of Sackler creatures and cousins
clamoring for a race war. *You're punching
down again,* I tell myself. I need directions

to that cardinal north where the Sunday lunch
is good on its own rather than an off-ramp
from my dossier of bullshit. More than that,
it's been years since I talked to someone

I called a neighbor, said anything more
than rugrat homilies or regurgitated
the temperature forecast. Whatever the real
Arkansas is, I've missed it. As I know to do,

I talk to the women about our children
but not ever to their husbands, fork a dog
into a bun and squeeze a line of ketchup
into its abiding valley. Have I driven past

miles of irrigated fields by the interstate,
blanched tufts in bloom, and acknowledged
their surface aesthetics before digging
into the carnage beneath? Our kids pump

the triggers on their impressive water guns,
as I compliment the tea for being sweet,
the dogs for being big, the people
for their kind invitation. Maybe it's all

I can do to live in limbo and call out
"not me" to no one listening, to nod at each
We're so glad you're here that rolls over me
like a blessing, unaware I had asked for it.

But for the hours I didn't care if I lived

At intervals I think
of what I don't give
my daughter, girl
who can't point
to a door frame,
her height scratched yearly
in pencil, as once I could.
I teach her spelling,
I watch her climb,
but she's scared of my office
at work, where I've sworn
to keep the door locked
so no one enters to shoot me,
as they do in the crime shows
I allow her to see.
Each time I fasten the door
I think of her. I've not
yet told my daughter
to fear my nights, that while
she sleeps I disappear
into a grave I create,
evening by evening,
cover myself
with punishing dirt,
laugh like a sorceress,
and the next day climb out.
I know she's confused
when she can't rouse me,
like the time I couldn't wake

my father after one of his
happy hours. I think of her,
usually, but for one night
when a friend had to call me
to keep me talking,
awake, ordered me
to go to the toilet and purge
the bitter liquid I drank.
Stomach finally empty,
I remembered my daughter
asleep under her frog blanket,
but for the hours
I didn't care if I lived,
I didn't know who or what
she was, person, child
in the next room. I return to
my father's heart,
how when a phone rang
long ago in my classroom
I knew it was time,
I had waited for this,
the click of my shoes
on institutional linoleum,
the principal speaking
in a low voice. But the call
was not for me. Dad was fine,
his death future tense.
Do we have children as a kind
of insurance, to guard
our minds like this, stop us
from ruining ourselves? I don't
deserve my daughter, still,
I feed her, I care

for her. After the hours
I didn't care if I lived,
I hugged her
and whispered in soothing tones.
I still do, promising not
to return to the place
I'd gladly have left her.

On this, our last day of the decade

my daughter coughs up flu
into the well of my palms. Later
I rub her back inelegantly,
her skinny little shaking bones.
For hours we alternate these
actions, and though I blame her
for my inactions,
equivocating in my mind
my own measured breath
to the blessing of tortures
both international and domestic,
inside all the stories I know,
the moral usually goes that
those who most benefit from evil
are troubled least, and look at
me. Mom in my forties, I cajole
the two-year-old inside me
with an economy of cookies
and milk, my ball-bearing
voice a skitter not a slap.
I have tried to be good.
I used to want to learn
to navigate systems, to see
our crisis as organized, but
I have marched to no effect,
and all my calls to Congress
die in voicemail. I'm afraid
as I watch our television, as
I consider figurations of power:

is power crushingly hard, or
shapeshifting so as to appear
harmless? Which?
I do not understand it.
No one smart has come up
with much of anything, and anyway,
the day draws me back—
our dryer broken, and my tire
flat, and her sick. On our
last day of the decade I knead
my girl's shoulders
as she cries into me
and I tell her to go again,
get it out. Get that sick out.

To be a mother in this economy

My child babies a squeeze bottle of craft glue
           or a lipstick tube filched from my purse.
She yanks a tissue from our coffee table

and spreads it out in the air, covers the baby,
           then balls up a second tissue to fluff
under its pretend head. They're all over the carpet,

babies. I want to help, but she motions me to go,
           shushes me. I find them everywhere,
rock baby, Matchbox baby, soapy baby

barrel of blow-bubbles. Sometimes
           she'll let me tuck her babies into our bed,
where they slumber alongside us, when I can,

when I'm with her. But I'm not always home,
           department store suit creased
into my luggage, phone jacked into an airport

wall, all those hotel stays hopeful for the job
           on the horizon, my baby in the care
of a friend. Sometimes the job came and we moved,

and my child learned to make friends and lose them,
           to shape her body to different earth
for a time, then say goodbye. I'm with her now,

I'm here, but I wonder if my absence lives inside
        her, if the babies are about that,
they are everything to her, these beloveds,

until she walks away.

Death parade

Standing over the hot oven I stir, arm turning spoon,
mind turning arm, making my daughter's meals. Call this

relief, the way the body knows to move forward
even as the mind scrolls. Everyone around me exhibits

bravery, if it's brave to Instagram your child's school project
during the pandemic death parade. I'm embarrassed

I once asked why the subjects of mad kings didn't rise up,
what it meant to nail parchment to a church door. Each day

I realize anew how elastic the mind is. I keep stretching
and stretching mine, repetitive motions like milking an udder

or pulling cloth through a machine, actions that kept
my ancestors alive. One day my mind will be large enough

to explain this to my daughter, but now, I offer the burlap
of my face for a kiss. We're free to walk outside, clean air,

the creekwater smells only a little of bleach. An upside, birds
alight everywhere, with glittering gem-cut eyes. She runs

through the landscape, unaware that this, too, can lift,
like the felt curtain of a failed middle school production

of *Our Town*. Did we do our best, *every, every minute?* Some think so,
old enough to have learned of the Great Depression in class,

turning it over in our minds but unable to see beyond
those aunts who sewed their own clothing, who used to frown

as they stewed and glass-jarred cardiac tomatoes
that we said were gross, that we swore we would not eat.

Baby care instructions

Before you lived, I lived inside my own
loathing. Some parents have children to replace
themselves, but we're two instead of none.
Pushing you on a swing, sunset, my hands
on your mammalian back, I remember
how everyone thought I'd kill you by mistake,
my throat in hives because I believed
them. You made me, too, daughter drawing
the last sip from a juicebox, wisps of hair
rising in the dirty breeze. I show you
how to kick to propel yourself, and all threat
dips like the sun behind the jungle gym.
I may have been born a knife, but my daughter
won't be a knife, nor its willing sheath.

In middle age, at last I understand

Dear literary dudebros,
dear lads of rock and roll,

I want to be rebellious
in a way nobody ever sang about.
I desire a removal of every language
I do not mean to speak
from my person, every other
person out of my body, out
of my blood and lungs and bile,
the limbs I thought worthless,
though in middle age I find them
worth a fortune. They really are,
although I reject the language
of value, too. You cannot
commerce me.

I enacted for too long what
other people wanted from me,
the fat purse of being wanted.
My lines lit me up. I took
direction, a girl taught
to acquire men but never
that the hilly lands I captured
had already been salted,
bare as the bald head of a queen.

It took me twenty years
but I stopped glistening.
I put the velvet away, the doe voice,

the shiny symmetry
under which I was dying.
Correction: I am getting closer
to dying all the time. I am getting
closer to mapping myself
as more than a territory to capture,
stuffed head for the hunter

to hang. I don't know—

is it better to cover up
or to shock an audience?
I may be cold marble now.
Or I might be on fire in the glow
of every dumb fable I told myself
combusting, over and over
like fireworks, my naked
breath blue like a torch.

What use are you?

In our final poetry class
my student says his parents who
pay for his education
are making him change his major,
that what I teach is of no use, and waits
for my protest. I am not the person
to ask. My god is so small,
he fits inside a Scantron sheet.
Each bubble opens like his mouth
to wail an ancient lament.
Actually, he is quiet.

According to a middle school test,
I should work in Administration.
Instead I am a teacher
in a school with few resources.
We took the test in the orchestra room,
among the ductwork and violins,
upright basses draped with dustcloths.
We had to carry our heavy instruments
to school and we did not complain.
We were in the art wing,
falling down, holes in the wall
where we crammed Wendy's wrappers
until the borders of the room fell in.

Projections will say we all need
nurses and HVAC techs and actuaries
but I was told by my parents
not to do those things and so today

I am quiet. I won't tell my student about
the law school where I almost
but didn't go because no one I knew
who went got an actual lawyering job.
This is a pyramid scheme
and for it to work
you've got to find out too late.
Some of my friends got Hospitality.
Some got Human Services. The best
got doctoral degrees we learned
to regret. The worst understood early
what "con man" is short for.

My student says he's switching
to Psych and when I ask why,
he looks despondent. My god
is so large he shakes the earth
in that imperceptible way that is simply
the earth moving. Ice melting.
Our heart-calving when the Provost
talks about cutting any program
that will not sustain itself.
The Provost is a kind man
but it is too late. We are finding out
what the verb means,
to use, and about the edges
on the noun, *use*, its humble slide
into the question
with our bodies at the end.

Forms and materials

Form is not

             my body, its bodily problems
by fortune a brief phone call or uncomplicated

doctor's visit. For years I dutifully followed
its directions, slotted limbs into the games

you may have tried, too, the blood-rust
carny rides and ball toss, bored fellow teen

at the helm. I didn't complain back then.
I needed affection like I deserved

to sit first-chair violin, to win the masonic
scholarship. In hooking up I earned a Fulbright.

For some sex is shameful, but like later
things I tried, drugging or extreme dieting,

this wouldn't be a big deal to me,
another example of socially condoned ways

to grow up. I don't know enough
about my ilk to call that normal,

but I sat in a lot of leatherette Hondas
making alpha, beta, and gamma plans to escape

being touched by boys. More than once,
an older woman asked if I knew what I was,

a dyke (she called herself), promising a slow
start, that we hold hands to get into the bar

since I was only 17. I didn't care—
I wanted to sit with someone, talk semiotics

or Japanese film, prime numbers, Anthony Bourdain—
and if a promise of sex got me close to that,

then okay.
                                    My body was an entrance fee

for women, too, though I got spooked back
to the boys who smelled like pot roast

and deodorant and would one day want kids.
I wanted a child, and like my math equations,

I knew what to do. You may have guessed,
I allowed but one way to do things.

–

Back then, I thought the only people
who understood "friend" as I did were long-gone

religious sects, Mennonites in cloisters
or the Shakers channeling lust into labor,

turning out sweaters, rocking chairs.

                                         What word

for me isn't ill-fitting, unclaimable?

                  A painter I know, a man
who gave birth around the same time I did

said we didn't have the language as teens
                              for what we are

and to me that made sense,

why he transitioned in his forties after a lifetime
of femme and why I can be honest now

about what the sex I had got me, a whack-
a-mole, a broken lease, a yeast infection?

For decades I argued with would-be and former
lovers but I always gave them   (mostly him)

what they wanted. I gave a kiss. A layover
in Saint Louis. A Sarah Lawrence girl

who spills her gimlet at last call pogoing
to the Stooges' *I wanna be your dog*

in an ex's memory. But who will I give
my honest answer to this: What *are* you, anyway?

                    Sir Talleyrand,
I read in the op-eds that The Future Isn't

Female Anymore,
but I'll still dedicate this volume to you—

I'm not a pronoun,
an orientation,   though I am that, too.

                        I am the word *continue*.

—

I am. I was. We were. I can't explain it to anyone
who once touched me except each time,

we were two people who bristled
and bubbled in exact specificity. Probably.

We had lives that formed us, these materials,
but marriage is terminally abstract

and so am I. I didn't want women or men, only an

                        ~ intellectual life ~

but instead I got chased from the dinner party
by some Puritan goody claiming I had designs

on her insipid mister, wrong idea,
but a clue to woman as domesticated pet

or wormy colonial acre. Until recently,
no credit without a husband's aye. Exiled,

I sat on the porch stoop or at Waffle House
spitting out a twisted little laugh

at being thought a slut, word like a glass bowl
refusing to break—ontologically incorrect,

irresponsible word. About his famous
character, the woman an A   awakened,

                         the male novelist wrote,
The world's law was no law for her mind.

Pain is always the vehicle, pain is feminine,
and for a while, I let anathema fill and vacate me,

an unsteady dot on the landscape, invisible
except to itself, flashing.

—

[Anecdote]
                                 Years ago, I visited—
provisionally—a womyn's commune nestled
in Southern hills I couldn't find now. The first
nonbinary person I knew, a new friend,
thought they'd live there. We ran our palms over
the tufted brows of goats and roved buttercup
hills all afternoon, then dined with the women,
their hair shorn or gathered in scarves, someone
inevitably picking at a guitar. A familiar situation,
mostly, transplants from Portland, New York.
The matriarch said she and her partner, a gay man,
built the place with their own hands. They'd
studied woodworking in books and were self-
taught farmers. All gathered at her long pine table
were some form of *separatist*—no straight men,
no one who consorts with men, a firm condition.
I pondered all of my gentle male exceptions

as we wound linguini to our mouths, plum tomatoes
and basil sprung from the farm's prolific garden,
the group performing human noises of satiety. Aware
I was a guest, I thanked the matriarch,
who said,
                    You don't get it yet, but you will,

and I said,
                    Oh, I do, I do get it,

but that was so long ago now and I am
just starting to. Perhaps, in the shadow

of Dobbs v. Jackson,
                    I could use some distance from men.

—

Some say my hand is simply *unasked for.*
As in: Dear sweet, please fit neatly

into our shared hetero void and behave
wife-like or we will fucking kill you

with celluloid and forced birth
and a fetus made into a god.

        Thy desire shall be to thy husband, and he shall rule over thee.

        *The very being and legal existence of the woman is suspended during
            the marriage, or at least is incorporated into that of her husband
                under whose wing and protection she performs everything.*

This hand is mine,

I scorn thy wing, I thrive in denial of thy desire,
nary hath struck me down.

Said another mother I know who'd had IVF:
        How ironic to pay a cryobank. I've had
        sperm in my bed,
        on my t-shirt, in my hair, everywhere . . .
        sperm, sperm, sperm.

There is too much sperm in America,
America is run by sperm,
                        but the vial I bought sprung me

from the Romance-Industrial Complex
that kept me docile for many years,

                and as an exit fee, it worked.

—

[Sonnet]
        You matter to me. Back in sex ed we saw
        genitals, breasts, sex organs. All else mere
        positioning, the way in. I prefer a voice,
        its kindness; a face, a custom tea set
        of expressions. Give me an acceptable
        love, not for everyone, but morphed to me.
        Its form could come in company or not,
        some purpose long stumbled over welling up
        suddenly. My daughter arrived by doctor's catheter;
        I didn't need sex at all. I still dream of friends
        who left, who didn't get it. Like my body,
        my dreams are rote, until I catch a blur

I recognize, and in the dark, my eyelids flutter.
A face or voice etched within me reaches out.

—

We've read already the story stitched
on my pelvis. Not born there, but worn anyway.

Only when I quit its familiar loop
of woe and wretchedness—as Mary W. put it,

My Life as a Toy of Man—could I testify
about the beckoning hand I anticipated,

conjuring children from air. The crone

peddling herbs at the forest perimeter
that villagers threaten to torch or stone

or mine for laughs on Twitter,
she midwifes all of the town's young,

crawls between caverns and surfaces
where new life blinks alive,
                              stunned. As I have.

Though an option, the Witch deflates me.
I hesitate to fold my ambition so neatly

into medieval Black Forest thinking,
that *Malleus* of woman-hating and -hunting

which still hacks out infinite decrees,
scrolls of punitive legislation,
                              judicial argument.

If form is shape and structure, I'm not
                              who or what I left out,

Mrs. Coney Barrett, I assure you—

no partner of mine is dead
            or in prison or simply too feckless
                        to keep loving me. Whispers

suggest I'm a casualty of women's lib,
            my girlhood a die to keep

casting. A perfect circle is hard to imagine
                        (except if you have imagination),

but it's obvious:
            my daughter and I are
            complete by ourselves. She is
                                                all capacity,

a bespoke miracle that learns easily,
as I once did, intuiting

her correct speed. Bit by bit I navigate rooms
with my voice, ambiguous walks

and calls at any hour to whoever I please,
a trip to the airport without significance,

to headline the bill, an act of *something*
                                                feline,
            something colubrine,

                        credible behavior
though it took me time to believe, too.

Recently on a hike, my friend asked after
My Life as a Drooping Lily (Mary W. again),

        meaning, why do I persist in such
glad self-liberation, and I said,

          I want to be able to talk to people
          without having to fuck or be fucked, yeah?

and with the flies whizzing around us,
the ticks burrowing into my socks

in midsummer, I said nothing else,
and she nothing, and we walked further

up the rock face, and I had stumped her
because that's all—the entire revolution so

                    painfully
simple—

     yet I refuse the lonely retreat,
to be swallowed by true crime podcasts

        and a day-drunk pinot,
though the hag-hairs on my chin

do blossom. Wield neither chainsaw
nor crockery, a holy conundrum—this blank

       will not fill,

but an example I set.

                 I'm found in front
of the auditorium,

applauding the ballet, the spelling bee,
a woman turned moral experiment,

                    A Wollstonecraft / A Moore
/ A Mother

hewn ride-or-die that birthed
        my open revolt of a girl, loyal

to my friends, we who chose something else. Now,

when the ellipsis pirouettes open
        its mutable door, beyond,

I find a new form, growing real. I call to her,

             Welcome home.

What if pain no longer ordered the narrative

Dinner, she pushes the triangles of French toast back and forth on her plate, forming amber currents of syrup, lifts a piece dripping to her mouth. I watch my daughter's jaw work as the restaurant clatters around us, an ordinary vortex of sound, and once again, I fix not on the object I love but on her taken, all standard-issue accidents, workaday shit, mostly crushed chassis and burnt-out wires. One of us will die first, and there are only two, no spare people. Such toxicity electrifies all of our meals, inaccessible, variable-thick, a theoretical her and a theoretical me, the only constant that I birthed her with a thirty-eight-year-old body, so those years divide us. In our pair, one will be left to singular loneliness on a future, unspecified day. This is absolutely true. But today she sips her milk from Styrofoam, her skull painted with white-blond hairs, blue beat of her pulse at the temple, a three-year-old with adult-sized ears. She'll replace me with another beloved one day, as children do, and if I don't let her, I'll fail, a different failure than those nights she'll bring me books to read when I'm too tired, or years of my tone poisoned by the inevitable fiascos at work, my entitlement pooling in our home like carbon monoxide. I've operated as a vassal in service to a terrible king for so long. Tonight I wrap her uneaten bacon to take with us and guide her arms to their jacket sleeves. I buckle her in. I don't groan at the train crossing. I allow another car to lurch into the lane ahead of us, and he flicks me the bird. In the rearview I watch my daughter's eyes, and I don't even curse the titans of industry who set America on fire.

On our street, I pull into the long coast of our driveway, the home I pray she'll think of fondly once I'm gone. Except I will never be gone. I carry her body inside, limp with sleep and curved against my shoulder, and I put her to bed.

Notes

No Spare People enacts a set of material realities bound by time, place, and social position with an interest in feminist theory. The perspective is limited by design. Thus, I chose epigraphs from *Living a Feminist Life* by Sara Ahmed (Duke University Press, 2017) and Adrienne Rich's "Notes Toward a Politics of Location" (from a lecture from the Conference on Women, Feminist Identity, and Society, 1984).

The epigraph from "The nineties" comes from an interview of Arundhati Roy published as "The Truth of Fiction" in the *San Francisco Chronicle*. I wrote this poem to interrogate how a very specific and privileged "I" and "we" understand the construction of historical events in present tense and in retrospect.

I have severe myopia, close to the limit of what can be surgically corrected. New lenses were implanted in my eyes after I finished writing this book. "If I wear glasses, will you be able to see me?" is based on a lifetime not seeing very well, at times dangerously so.

In aughts-era messageboard vernacular, self-owning (or self-pwning) referred to a post that makes a fool of its author ("Self-owning rondeau").

I couldn't have written "The power of passive voice" without all of the information about Reality Winner I read in Kerry Howley's *New York* article, "Who is Reality Winner?" Winner was transferred from prison to a transitional facility in 2021.

Much of the historical information in "Retail requiem" comes from *Penn Live*'s "Stores from our past we miss: Ames, Pomeroy's, Jamesway and more" by Daniel Urie, but I did my own research, too. My family shopped and worked in these places.

"Maternity exhibit as the singularity" is one of a series of maternity exhibit poems that I wrote. Per Merriam Webster, the event horizon is the boundary of a black hole. Nothing can escape from within it.

A proof of impossibility demonstrates that a particular problem, such as the speaker's own sexuality, can't be solved as described in the claim ("Proof of impossibility").

In "Real Arkansas," I extend the vernacular "invited to the cookout" to any kind of belonging that requires entering into historical and ongoing power dynamics.

Emily Webb speaks the line in Thornton Wilder's *Our Town* referenced in "Death parade": "Oh, earth, you're too wonderful for anybody to realize you. Do any human beings ever realize life while they live it — every, every minute?"

In "Forms and materials," I use the concept of Platonic forms to depict my years-long reaching for a gendered ideal that I could accept as authentic (at least provisionally) during our era of prescriptive—even toxic—models of the feminine. Quotations on marriage are from Genesis 3:16 and *Commentaries on the Laws of England* by William Blackstone, and I have also used snippets from Nathaniel Hawthorne's novel *The Scarlet Letter*, "Marriage" by Marianne Moore, and Mary Wollstonecraft's "A Vindication of the Rights of Women."

Acknowledgments

Thank you to the editors who have read my work with generosity. Poems from this manuscript have appeared in:

Bennington Review: "The hedge fund manager's first wife"

Cincinnati Review: "Apartment home in Florida as failure of the imagination"

Cortland Review: "Visiting assistant professor"

Couplet: "Homewrecker," "Proof of impossibility"

Crazyhorse: "Self-owning rondeau"

Florida Review: "White woman"

Gargoyle: "The nineties," "The power of passive voice," "What use are you?"

Northwest Review: "Forms and materials" (excerpt)

On the Seawall: "Praying inside the emergency," "Retail requiem," "Three weeks"

Plume: "On this, our last day of the decade"

Poetry Northwest: "Maternity exhibit in an election year," "Maternity exhibit as the singularity"

Prairie Schooner: "Death parade"

Shenandoah: "On the metaphor, for women, of birthing to creative activity," "At the child support office," "Baby care instructions"

Split This Rock: "To be a mother in this economy"

The Sun: "What if pain no longer ordered the narrative"

"Baby care instructions" is anthologized in *Mid/South Sonnets* (Belle Point Press, 2023).

"Retail requiem" will be anthologized in *Keystone: Contemporary Poets on Pennsylvania* (Penn State University Press, 2025).

I wish to thank Rebecca Morgan Frank and Sandy Longhorn as early readers of these poems. Thank you, Cate Marvin, Kaveh Akbar, K. Iver, and Jessica Jacobs for championing *No Spare People*, and C.T. Salazar and Lauren Cerand for your good ideas. I wrote these poems at the Hambidge Center and the Writers' Colony at Dairy Hollow, and in academic positions at Hendrix College and Tennessee Tech. I remain truly grateful for those communities. For parents, especially mothers, it is difficult to write without caregivers, and this book only exists because of Arin Barger, Jennifer Esper, and George and Cheryl Hoover. Ever Baldwin and Lee Folmar, your friendships have saved my life over and over again. Dear Hester, all my books are for you.

Photo: Keistryn Steward

Erin Hoover is the author of a previous poetry collection, *Barnburner*, which won Elixir Press's Antivenom Poetry Award and a Florida Book Award. Originally from Pennsylvania, she lives in rural Tennessee and teaches creative writing at Tennessee Tech University.